Stars

By John Lockyer

Stars can be seen at night.

3

A red dwarf

A giant

Our sun is a yellow dwarf.

Stars are different sizes.
Large stars are called giants
or supergiants.
Smaller stars are called dwarfs.

A supergiant

Stars are different colors.
They can be red, yellow, blue, or white.

The Sun
(yellow)

Sirius
(white)

Betelgeuse
(red)

Vega
(blue)

Stars are made in clouds
of very hot gas.

Places where stars are being made

Stars grow bigger and redder
as the gas burns up.
Then they shrink
to small white dwarf stars.

A white dwarf

A red giant

Some giant stars explode
at the end of their lives.
They are called supernovas.

A Single Star

The Sun is a single star.

A Double Star

A red giant

A white dwarf

There are stars by themselves.
There are pairs of stars called double stars.

14

A spiral galaxy

Large groups of stars are called galaxies.

There are lots and lots of galaxies
in the universe.